Pegs and Socks

Written by Clare Helen Welsh
Illustrated by Paul Nicholls

Collins

Seb has big socks.

2

3

Socks go up and off!

Seb runs.

5

Seb pegs up the socks.

Seb huffs.

huff, huff

Socks go up and off!

Seb runs.

Seb huffs and Seb puffs.

Seb picks up the pegs.

Seb pegs up the socks!

13

14

After reading

Letters and Sounds: Phase 2

Word count: 56

Focus phonemes: /b/ /f/, ff

Common exception words: and, go, the, has

Curriculum links: Understanding the World: People and Communities; The World

Early learning goals: Reading: read and understand simple sentences; use phonic knowledge to decode regular words and read them aloud accurately; read some common irregular words; demonstrate understanding when talking with others about what they have read

Developing fluency

- Encourage your child to sound talk and then blend the words e.g. p/e/g. It may help to point to each sound as your child reads.
- Then ask your child to reread the sentence to support fluency and understanding.
- Have fun reading the speech bubbles using different voices. Can you use a cross voice? Can you whisper? Can you use a deep voice or a squeaky voice?

Phonic practice

- Ask your child to sound talk and blend each of the following words: s/o/ck/s, h/u/ff/s, r/u/n/s.
- Look through the book together. Can your child find words with the "ck" sound in? (*socks, picks*)
- Look at the "I spy sounds" pages (14–15). Discuss the picture with your child. Can they find items/ examples of words that include the /f/ and /ff/ sounds? (*fizzy drink, fish, food, fruit, fork, frog, flower, fire, sniff, toffee, falling off (the peas are falling off the spoon)*)

Extending vocabulary

- Ask your child:
  - Seb huffs and puffs. What words can you use to describe how he is feeling? (e.g. *angry, cross, annoyed, mad*)
  - Seb runs after the socks. What other words could you use instead of **runs**? (e.g. *jogs, bounces, treks, jumps, goes*)